Dave –
More onus Having
Kev's to Insure

FOLLOW THE MONEY

in Upstate New York!

J[signature]

FOLLOW THE MONEY

How to Go From Insurance Agent to Wealthy Insurance Entrepreneur and Live the Lifestyle of Your Dreams On Your Terms

JOHN MASON, CIC

Copyright 2019 John Mason

ALL RIGHTS RESERVED. This book contains material protected under International and Federal Copyright Laws and Treaties. Any unauthorized reprint or use of this material is prohibited. No part of this book may be reproduced or transmitted in any form or by any means, electronic or mechanical, including photocopying, recording, or by any information storage and retrieval system, without express written permission from the author/publisher.

ISBNs:

Paperback
978-1-64184-054-5

Ebook
978-1-64184-055-2

TABLE OF CONTENTS

INTRODUCTION 1

1) DIRTY LITTLE SECRETS I'VE LEARNED ABOUT
BUYING INSURANCE AGENCIES & BROKERAGES 5

2) HOW TO GET APPOINTED BY THE CARRIERS YOU
WANT BY GIVING THEM WHAT THEY WANT 13

3) BROKER FEES: THE TICKET TO WEALTH OR AN
INVITATION TO THE COMMISSIONER'S OFFICE? 17

4) SUREFIRE RETENTION STRATEGIES TO KEEP YOUR
CLIENTS LOVING YOU – AND SENDING YOU
MONEY FOREVER AND A DAY 19

5) 'TIL DEATH DO YOU (AND YOUR CLIENTS) PART –
ADVANCED TIPS ON CLIENT NURTURING 25

6) MAKE YOUR PHONES RING LIKE CHURCH BELLS ON STEROIDS WITH THE FREE PUBLICITY MACHINE THAT'LL HAVE THE MEDIA EATING OUT OF YOUR PALM ... 31

7) WHEN YOUR COMPETITOR JUST WON'T QUIT AND HOLDS ONTO CANCEL REQUESTS LIKE A ROTTWEILER ON A BONE ... 35

8) GETTING YOUR AGENCY READY TO SELL TO THE HIGHEST BIDDER, LONG BEFORE THAT FIRST SHOVEL OF DIRT HITS YOU IN THE FACE ... 39

9) HOW TO FIRE A CLIENT…LEGALLY ... 43

10) HOW TO HELP THE LESS FORTUNATE IN YOUR COMMUNITY, GET NEW PROSPECTS IN YOUR FRONT DOOR, MASSIVE FREE PUBLICITY AND LOOK LIKE A HERO ALL OVER TOWN ... 47

11) HOW TO USE TESTIMONIALS IN YOUR BUSINESS? ... 55

12) FIRST IMPRESSIONS COUNT! HERE'S HOW TO BOOST YOUR CLOSING RATIO, SHOCK & AWE YOUR PROSPECT AND IMPRESS THE HECK OUT OF YOUR CARRIERS! ... 59

13) WHEN CLIENTS LEAVE, YOU DON'T HAVE TO BE LIKE LITTLE BO PEEP AND HER SHEEP! HERE'S HOW… ... 63

14) USING PERSONALITY MARKETING TO FILL YOUR FUNNEL WITH LEADS, YOUR CSRS DESKS WITH NEW APPS YOUR BANK ACCOUNT WITH COLD HARD CASH 67

15) NOW THAT YOU'VE DISCOVERED TESTIMONIALS YOU CAN KICK BUTT WITH THEIR BIG BROTHER! INTRODUCING THE THIRD-PARTY ENDORSEMENT LETTER! 71

16) IF ONLY YOUR AGENCY WAS LIKE THE HOTEL CALIFORNIA: CLIENTS WOULD CHECK-IN AND NEVER LEAVE! 75

17) WANT TO POUR YOUR PROFITS DOWN THE TOILET, SET UP A COMPETITOR IN YOUR OWN AGENCY, AND LATER SCRATCH YOUR HEAD WONDERING, "WHY THE HELL DID I DO THAT?" HERE'S HOW… 79

ABOUT THE AUTHOR 85

INTRODUCTION

Thirty years ago I went into the insurance business in a small town in rural upstate New York. The deck was stacked against me as had I started my business in a very poor rural town with not much of an economic base. I had no direct appointments, no experience, and no money. While I was accepted in a business administration program at a major northeastern university, I chose not to go to college. Instead, I stayed in my small town, started a family, and struggled financially as I started various businesses and finally "fell into" insurance. The early years were tough, but the reward for all this hard work was over-the-top.

There were many sleepless nights when I would drive to the office at 2:00 in the morning to figure out what checks might be clearing that day. We had a young family, struggled financially, and almost lost our house to foreclosure. After a couple of years,

I was fortunate enough to pick up a great New York-based regional carrier and a top-rated national carrier and things began to fall into place.

Then the work began, and I did it the hard way.

My marketing strategy, while it worked well financially, made me a slave to my business, but at that point, I knew of no other way. I'd run classified and display ads in community papers and "penny-savers" telling people about other people who had saved money by switching to my agency. The calls would come in, and I'd spend many evenings at kitchen tables explaining how home and auto policies worked, signing applications (that someone had typed during the day), taking pictures with a Polaroid Instamatic camera. Then, the major national carrier I represented decided to go into non-standard auto, appointed me in a couple of states, and I went wild. I stepped up the ads and was soon meeting six to eight new customers (not clients) in the early morning and weekends in McDonald's parking lots everywhere within 100 miles of my office to write non-standard auto insurance off the trunk of my used Cadillac.

Things began to get better. An opportunity came along to buy another agency in the area and fold it into my existing agency, and these opportunities kept coming. In 1997, we built an office building, and when I asked the builder why he designed a building much bigger than I needed, he grinned and said, "Don't worry, you'll grow into it and do things with your business you never imagined."

While the building was being built, I got the opportunity to buy a small wholesale brokerage in my area that focused on rural property and personal auto in upstate NY. We immediately began moving it into other parts of the state, then other states, and suddenly we are now in 20 states. In 2007, we had the opportunity to buy a non-standard auto shop right next door to the only Department of Motor Vehicles in the Bronx. Over the next four years, I'd buy four more brokerages in the Bronx and one more upstate. I began selling off the retail agencies a few years ago and have focused strictly on growing my wholesale brokerage.

There are many people I need to thank for their contributions along the way. I could never have done this without the incredibly smart, hard-working and dedicated team of professionals who have worked for the organization over the years and many of them are still with us. My family has been ultra-supportive, enduring all those years I was absent and working, but all fully aware now of the benefits it would eventually bring.

To Dad, thank you for being there all those Fridays when I didn't have the money to cover payroll and for being there as my short-term bank. I know you'd be proud of all that has happened, and thank you for believing in me.

I'd also be remiss not to thank all of the brokers who have trusted in us over the years. Without your undying support of Chenango Brokers, this book would never have needed to be written. I also want to thank all of the agents and other professionals I have worked with at carriers and other industry trade and marketing groups over the years. What I've learned from many of you has been priceless.

Over the past few months, I have compiled a series of short articles based on my experiences, lessons, failures, and successes. May this book show you some shortcuts to success, detours around the trouble spots, and the path toward the kind of success our industry has showered upon me.

Read this now, and God help your competition.

John N. Mason
January 2019

CHAPTER 1
DIRTY LITTLE SECRETS I'VE LEARNED ABOUT BUYING INSURANCE AGENCIES AND BROKERAGES

Business has been good. Sales are up. Claims activity is low. Retention gets better each month. You've almost spent next year's contingency three times in your head and have visions of your family enjoying that little vacation you keep imagining. *But if business is good, wouldn't another agency make it even better?*

I often hear agents say that they'll *"just ask the marketing rep who's for sale the next time they stop in."* Don't bet the ranch on that one. Of course, after a friendly visit to your agency, he'll close with some non-obligatory line promising to let you know if he hears something. Yeah, right, and I've got forty acres of prime swamp land in Mississippi that I'll give you a smokin' deal on, too. Do you honestly believe that if you're one of his or her smaller agents that you'll get that call? No. When he comes upon that juicy little tidbit, he's gonna race to his car and call one of your larger competitors; you know, the one he plays golf with while you're out struggling to make a buck to pay your bills. Maybe a bottle of expensive wine, dinner, use of his vacation home, a plane ticket, or some other little gift will quietly change hands, but you won't be part of the equation, mark my word.

Before you run out and drop half-a-gazillion on another agency, you should ask yourself some questions, such as:

- If I buy another agency, how will my existing agency be impacted?

- Will the acquisition give me bigger books of business with some of my existing carriers and increase contingency potential?

- What carriers does the other agency represent that I would like to represent?

- What niches, if any, does the other agency work in? Do I understand and have a passion for those niches?

- Can I merge the other agency into (one of) my existing location(s)?

- Has the agency run into any legal problems, terminations, or financial issues that you might be aware of?

Then I identified a list of agencies in the areas we did business in that I wanted to buy. Then I created a marketing campaign aimed right at those agencies. (Heck, they know I understand marketing, just based on all the clients I have taken from them). I started out with a letter introducing myself and the fact that I buy agencies. If I saw something in trade publications that I thought might impact their agency or one of their carriers, I'd clip it and mail it over with a handwritten note to the owner.

But the bait that made the fish bite was the handwritten letter (maybe written by me) and signed by an agency principal I had bought out for cash a couple years earlier. The letter, "handwritten" on a piece of 8½ x 11, yellow, lined paper with blue ink went on and on about the rat race and day-to-day hassle of running an agency. Then it talked about this guy (describing me) who had been writing to him for ages wanting to buy the agency, and I came along and put bags of money in his pocket. For good measure, the "handwritten" letter (printed commercially in my own handwriting) was crumpled, dribbled with coffee stains, and placed in a vinyl bank deposit bag (from Amazon) with a couple generous handfuls of shredded money (available from the Feds). The money bag became the mailing envelope and had both my unique nine-digit return address and a hand-written address label on the front. Postage was less than $3 and the total cost of the mailer somewhere around six bucks, but it made agents reach out to me when they were ready to sell.

Whatever method you use to contact prospective acquisitions, be sure to give them direct and confidential ways to reach you. Yes, your cell phone, private email, home phone, etc., because when they call you, it won't be to talk about your golf game or last night's Red Sox game. It will be business, and they do not want the whole world to know they're calling you. They won't want you coming to or calling the office or being seen with you having lunch until the deal is done and over.

So, the day comes that you're scheduled to meet, and after you get through the uncomfortable small talk, most of them will ask you that God-awful question:

"What multiple are you currently paying for agencies?"

"Well, gollllly, Sargent Carter, I don't know..."

Never get pinned into answering this question from a potential seller. Instead, tell them that you "utilize a few valuation methods including gross (commission) revenue as well as an EBITDA calculation of the last three years" to come up with an offer that is affordable for you but puts the most money possible in their pocket.

"When I take all of your numbers back, I'll start working on that." You dodged his question honestly, and just let him know that you're going to want to see his books. I won't get into specific multiples of sales or EBITDA because the numbers will vary drastically depending on many factors including but not limited to whether or not you'd merge this business into an existing location or run it separately. Shelter cost, like labor cost, is very expensive. You'll want to calculate EBITDA both on the existing business, and also how that business will perform under your model, whether stand-alone or merged into your office. Shelter and labor costs are super-expensive. Don't let your ego convince you that you need more locations than necessary.

"I'm not holding any paper. I want cash, and I'm heading to The Villages to . . . ."

You probably could care less about what he plans to do when he rolls into God's Waiting Room in Central Florida in his Winnebago, and I certainly don't want the visual, but there's a way around this one too, and I've done it a few times. For round number's sake, let's say you and the seller agree on a purchase price of $100,000, and he wants cash on the barrelhead. You know you could offer a retention arrangement or owner financing with a healthy down payment, but you also know he wants cash and will take less money if he can get it. Go to your bank and give them the $100,000 in the form of a CD or whatever you negotiate for them to then turn around and loan you back 100 cents on the dollar of the cash you gave them as collateral. At the end of the financing period, you own the agency free and clear, have paid the bank some tax-deductible interest, and you get your hundred grand back from the bank!

You need professional help. Seriously.

So, you've come to terms with Retiring Rick, your-soon-to-be-ex-competitor, and you want to get his signature on a contract as soon as you can before word gets out and one of your other not-so-friendly-competitors shows up with a bigger offer. Do not call your attorney unless he or she has experience in buying and selling agencies. There are several aspects to an agency acquisition that are very specific, and these can run from carrier appointment contingencies, how unearned commissions are handled, producer contracts and ownership of books, employment issues, and more. I consider my own attorney to be an expert at this based on the number of deals he has done for me and the purchase contract he has developed over many years of acquiring agencies for me. Please don't ask me for a copy of his agreement as you'll get to see it if you retain him.

A strong CPA, with experience in this area, is also crucial and will help you decide how to allocate the asset purchase, corporate structure, etc.

A few tidbits I've learned:

- If the seller doesn't own the building or you will not be utilizing that location, lease the space for a while to keep signage in it directing clients to your office. Wouldn't it be a shame if you moved and a competitor moved in? One time I almost bought a competitor's office right out from under him; you have to be very careful.

- Employees are an issue. Do any of the staff or producers own their books? Are there any special deals in place with staff? Have any promises been made that you need to be aware of? Anyone there who plans to leave and start their own agency and they don't have a covenant not to compete?

- After the closing, you need to notify the clients. I've found the best way to do that is a letter from the former agent with a picture of him handing you the keys standing in front of the office. Maybe have the staff in this picture too. Will he be sticking around as a consultant for a while?

- How do the wages in this agency compare with the wages you pay your own staff, and will you need to make adjustments?

- Are you buying the assets or the corporation, and do you understand the risks you run if you purchase the entity?

These are just a few of the things I learned over the years as I acquired a dozen agencies or books of business. While I don't know it all, I sure hope that my experiences can work to your advantage.

CHAPTER 2
HOW TO GET APPOINTED BY THE CARRIERS YOU WANT BY GIVING THEM WHAT THEY WANT

So, you've decided you're ready to add a carrier to the lineup of companies in your portfolio. You call the marketing rep, set up an appointment, he comes to your office, you talk some more, go to lunch, and he reminds you of what he needs from you to take back to the home office to try to get your appointment underwritten. You shake hands, promise to get it all to him next week, and . . .

Your receptionist hands you seven phone messages, your email box has blown up, your best CSR left during lunch to go to Susie's volleyball tournament, three referral sources have leads for you, the claim on your golf partner's "missing" Rolex just got sent to SIU, and your mother-in-law is texting because her car insurance went up three dollars a month, and she never liked you in the first place.

Day after day, another batch of problems, and it goes on and on. Three weeks go by, and you've forgotten all about Smiling Sam from Quick Sand Mutual and the information he needed for your appointment. He's called and emailed you a few times and has now more or less given up on you.

Sound familiar? There's a much easier way.

This is where your *Bullseye Agency Appointment Kit* comes into play. This is where you shine and leave Smiling Sam wondering how you did it, his bosses wondering why more agents don't do it, and you ready to sign the contract. You should already have all of the information to build this readily available in your office and can assemble a few copies of your *Bullseye Agency Appointment Kit*. Here's a list of ingredients to make this work:

- Clear picture of your agency location(s)
- Clear, preferably professional, photos of yourself and all key staff
- Agency Mission Statement
- Testimonial sheet from your agency
- Third-party endorsement letter

HOW TO GET APPOINTED BY THE CARRIERS YOU WANT

- Biography of yourself and of each key staff member
- Copies of licenses yourself, licensed personnel, and the agency in each state you're seeking an appointment
- Copy of your current E&O declarations page
- Copy of a W-9 for your agency
- Copies of your most current production and loss reports from each of your carriers. If the current report doesn't include the three most recent year-end reports, include those too.
- While it would be great to include your marketing plans, this information is strategic and proprietary, and you certainly wouldn't want it falling into the hands of a competitor. Do not include it.

Arrange all of the information in an orderly fashion in a loose-leaf notebook or even a PDF. I recommend loose leaf because you're giving ole Smilin' Sam something tangible to take back to his boss, and more importantly, as you get updated production and loss reports, E&O decs, etc., you can update your book.

When you invest the little bit of time required to do this, you'll set yourself apart from all the agents who have no time management skills and allow the interruptions of day-to-day agency life to prevent them from securing companies, growing their agencies, and having those agencies run on autopilot.

CHAPTER 3
BROKER FEES: THE TICKET TO WEALTH OR AN INVITATION TO THE COMMISSIONER'S OFFICE?

For the last twenty years or so, I've been hanging around the water coolers of some fantastic trade groups for agency owners. These could be agent organizations, marketing companies who bring like-minded agents together, continuing ed classes, or even some of the great online principal forums that exist today.

One topic that always comes up is fees. How much should I charge? Is it legal in my state? (Are you sure?) Can I charge for certificates and payments? (If I do, do I need a new fee acknowledgment form?) I'm an agent of Sinking Sands Mutual; am I allowed to charge fees? How much do you charge? And of course the braggarts, usually from one coast or the other, who can't wait to rub it in how much they charged on some hard-to-place EPLI for Hollywood's latest movie-star-gone-afoul.

The first bit of advice I would give you is to make sure that if you are going to charge fees, you do it in full compliance of the law of the state(s) the risk is in. If you're not sure, contact the state's regulatory arm for insurance agents and brokers and ask. They would much rather have you do that than charge fees illegally or improperly. Regulators are not likely to be sympathetic toward producers who charge fees in a manner non-compliant with the law. National Underwriter publishes a book each year that lists current licensing and fee regulations for each state.

If you work exclusively for one carrier, such as captive agent carriers, in addition to making sure that you can legally charge fees, you should also make sure that the practice has the blessing of your carrier.

The laws vary from state-to-state. Some states have a set schedule of what you can charge and the reasons for doing so. Other states don't allow fees at all. Other states, such as New York, will allow a broker (who represents the insured) to charge a fee, but an agent (who represents a carrier) may not. It is also a requirement that the insured sign an acknowledgment of any fee he has paid, which is likely to be the case in most states. If you sell both property and casualty as well as life products, make sure that you check state laws to see if the regulations vary between the products.

CHAPTER 4
SUREFIRE RETENTION STRATEGIES TO KEEP YOUR CLIENTS LOVING YOU – AND SENDING YOU MONEY FOREVER AND A DAY

Over the years, you've built a successful agency, made an incredible living, collected obscene contingency checks, gone on some incredible trips with the carriers, the money is rolling in, and your spouse has finally stopped nagging you about bills.

Life is good. Then, one night you're sitting on the couch, wearing those hideous polka-dotted sweats that Aunt Gladys re-gifted to you four Christmases ago, watching re-runs of *Law & Order*, when it hits you like a ton of bricks.

First, it's that fast-talking obnoxious lizard or his friend the pig. Then comes that bimbo in the white coat who works for that carrier you represent who would love to have you believe they aren't your competitor. Next comes Jake, in his khakis, who's just dying for you to go to bed so he can call your wife and whisper sweet nothings to her about percentage deductibles. And to top it all off that dirty-old-man with the bad mustache comes across the boob-tube hawking low-end car insurance.

Not only are you watching this endless parade of bad actors peddling cut-rate and cut-coverage car insurance, so are your customers. And they believe this nonsense.

You sit there in your polka dots thinking, *I'm protected from all that. After all I do for my customers, they'll stay with me forever. I've donated to their Little League fundraisers, eaten those awful pancakes the Lions Club pushes one Sunday a month, bought endless Girl Scout cookies and enough over-priced popcorn to keep Orville Redenbacher drooling in his rocking chair for decades. Yeah, my clients will stick around forever."* Right. And, I'll sell you 1,200 acres of prime swamp land in Florida too.

And it's everywhere you turn: newspapers, the Internet, magazines, TV, radio. Even billboards in places like Post Falls, Idaho.

That is NOT how your clients see it. You see, the marketing wizards behind these giant money-sucking machines have convinced the vast majority of the

American public that the only thing one should judge an insurance carrier on is how low their pricing is. Not one bloody other thing, and your customers are sucking this in hook, line, and sinker.

Don't throw in the towel just yet. You can protect your agency from this endless barrage of fake news. You see, these big, rich, greedy direct writers know that most agents don't market to their existing clients once the new business deposit check has cleared. Yes, Virginia, there is a Santa Claus, and I'm here to help you protect your clients (and your retention ratio) from this den of thieves.

You see, marketing cannot stop the minute you sign the client up. In fact, it takes a bit of a turn and continues in a different path once the prospect sees the light and becomes a client. It's your job to turn him or her into a raving fan, referral machine, and a client for life.

Here are some of the things I did over the years in my agencies.

Random handwritten notes thanking your clients for their business. I am not talking about Send-Out-Cards or some other computer-generated message. Pick up your damned pen and scratch out eight or ten of these every day. Your clients will truly appreciate getting these and will see them as a sincere gesture, unlike getting a computer-generated font in the mail. Think about it; when was the last time you got a thank-you note from the owner of a business you patronize?

Safety tips show your clients that you care (and simultaneously help protect your loss ratio). For example, you can email or send a broadcast voicemail to your clients a few days before Thanksgiving to, for Pete's sake, not drop a 25-pound frozen turkey into a gallon of hot grease in the middle of the kitchen (or anywhere close to a structure for that matter). Or maybe a few days before Halloween, you can send a message about keeping sidewalks and steps clear and well-lit and locking Killer the Rottweiler up when the little chocolate-sucking ghosts and goblins are banging on their front door.

Newspaper clippings are fantastic excuses to reach out and touch your clients. People still read local community papers, so subscribe to them in the towns you serve. Clip articles and pictures you see about your clients and their families. Watch for kids' sports and school awards, job promotions, birth announcements, weddings, or fun news stories. (Probably a good idea to stay away from obits and the police notes). Clip the articles, and laminate them along with an ad from your agency ("Look Who's In the News! Congratulations from all your friends at the Mason Agency.") Attach a strip of magnetic tape and mail it out with a quick handwritten note.

Birthday greetings. The most important day of the year to most people is their birthday. Come up with a unique way to wish your clients a happy birthday. Be creative and come up with something better than a card, such as a video greeting from the staff, a phone call, a personalized gift sent to work, etc.

Calendars, and I don't mean the standard pre-done jobs that you get samples of every November. When you take pictures of your clients' houses and cars during the course of the year, store them electronically and then drop them into a one-page calendar on card-stock. Mail these out just after January 1 so they don't get tossed out along with all the phony corporate Christmas cards that flood their mailboxes in December. Your calendar with a picture of their home or car or toy will get displayed and shown to everyone they know, and probably shared all over social media, too.

There are so many other things you can do like newsletters, emails, postcards, etc., and all are good, but I've devoted this space to things that not every other business in town is doing. Be different. Be bold. Be in front of your clients in ways nobody else is, and you will keep them for a very long time to come.

Those magnetic laminated clippings immediately get stuck on refrigerators all over your area, and when their friends visit, they see the clipping as well as an advertisement for your agency.

CHAPTER 5
'TIL DEATH DO YOU (AND YOUR CLIENTS) PART – ADVANCED TIPS ON CLIENT NURTURING

The secret to keeping clients is to keep in touch with them regularly. Little touches, not long diatribes that won't be read, or pitches designed to line your pocket with more dollars. Soft, easy touches to let them know you're looking out for them and that you care will glue them to your agency.

God knows the direct writers and their fat-pocket budgets are spending a ton of money to reach out and touch YOUR clients!

There are a number of things you can do nurture your clients, and many of them are free. Others cost very little, and most of the rest of them won't break the bank.

Here are my Top Ten Client Nurturing Tricks designed to get your clients to stick with you through thick and thin, insulate them from the low-cost cutthroat direct writers, and keep your retention rate higher than a kite.

1. Marketing does not stop the day the client signs the application. In fact, this is when you kick it into high gear. The first three weeks of your relationship with your new client will set the tone forever. My advice is to hit them immediately with a hand-written thank-you note from you, the owner of the agency. A week later, a welcome kit that can include a directory of who to call in your agency, direct-claim reporting number and websites, free gifts with your agency name on it, an intro to your referral program, white papers on other products, etc. Maybe the third step is a note from the CSR assigned to their account letting them know he/she is licensed and can handle all of their customer service needs, and that he/she has the same license as you do so they never need to wait for you to get back to them. (You just set delegation and time management expectations into play in a friendly way).

2. A successful agent-friend of mine in California recently posted in an agent forum that he sent

out thank-you cards to his first 500 clients (he's been around awhile and has thousands of clients now). People like to be recognized and thanked. Not only will this cement long relationships, but it will also garner more than a few referrals for your agency.

3. The most important day of the year. Hint: It is not the day the marketing rep from your top carrier walks in with your bonus check. Everyone has a birthday, and a card from your agency, maybe an email, a touch on social media, or all three will be appreciated. Another idea is a "what happened on the day you were born" printout from the Internet. Be careful not to violate any state rebating laws if you send gifts as most states have limitations on how much you can give away.

4. Your newsletter, whether monthly or quarterly, is your chance to nurture clients, recognize referral sources, promote client reward contests, recognize staff, cross-sell, up-sell, offer safety tips, recognize clients who have gone out of their way to help others, and much more. Many agents are tempted to send this by email, but I always preferred using direct mail as it is a tangible delivered to the front door. While everyone else is using email, turn around and run in the opposite direction. Just think how little direct mail you get in your own mailbox each day and how effective a friendly newsletter from your team could be.

5. While the daily papers are struggling to maintain ad revenue and subscribers, the community newspapers are thriving. People love to read about their friends and neighbors in the paper. Subscribe to all the community papers in the towns where you have clients, clip anything (positive) about your clients and their kids and grandkids and laminate them. When you laminate, also include a colorful note at the top that says, "Look Who's in the News! Congratulations from Your Friends at XYZ Agency." Put some magnetic tape on the back of the laminated piece, and, presto, you just created an advertisement for your agency that they'll stick on their refrigerator for all their friends and family to see. (It's probably a good idea not to scan the police notes on this one or send a clipping of Crazy Uncle George getting his third DWI arrest.)

6. Send safety tips by email. If there's a hurricane, earthquake, winter storm, power outage, or other such catastrophe approaching an area where your clients are, send free tips to keep your clients (and your loss ratio) safe. An agent friend in Buffalo frequently does this to warn of weather conditions, closings, what to do in a claim, or even if he needs to close his office for such an emergency. I'm on his mailing list, and even if I wasn't in the insurance business, I sure like getting these and knowing he and his agency are looking out for me. If you use services like ringless voicemail, you can

implement these too, but as always, be very careful not to violate FCC regulations.

7. Insurance is as boring as watching grass grow. Make it fun! If there's a concert, sporting event, culinary event, etc., going on in an area where your clients are, pick up a couple tickets and raffle them off to your clients. Make it fun yet beneficial to your agency. Email your client list that you have tickets and that you'll give them away for FREE to the 27th (or whatever number) client to post a testimonial on your website or Facebook page stating how your agency has helped them. Make sure you make it clear no additional purchase is necessary and that by doing so, you can use their testimonial in your marketing.

8. Social media is more than scrolling to get the gossip, although you do pick up some juicy tidbits. An agent friend of mine in Syracuse routinely promotes his commercial clients' businesses on his Facebook page. It advertises that commercial client's business to his other clients and really helps solidify his relationship with his commercial clients, too.

9. When you give away things to your clients, be smart about it. First, make sure you are compliant with state laws in the area you're doing this. Second, support your clients. Unless you insure restaurants such as Applebee's, Chili's or Outback, buy gift certificates only from locally-owned restaurants that you insure.

You're supporting your clients' businesses and introducing them to new customers in the form of your clients. My friend in Syracuse takes it a step further and has an arrangement with his client-restaurants that he doesn't pay for the gift certificate unless/until it is used.

10. If you do community service projects, and you should, involve your clients and recognize them. I won't re-write the whole playbook here but look at our food bank project, created by yet another agent friend, in Ontario. It helps the needy, involves community service organizations, and recognizes clients, staff, and all who participate in it.

CHAPTER 6
MAKE YOUR PHONES RING LIKE CHURCH BELLS ON STEROIDS WITH THE FREE PUBLICITY MACHINE THAT'LL HAVE THE MEDIA EATING OUT OF YOUR PALM

Please don't take the meaning of this paragraph wrong, but when something goes wrong, it's your chance to show up like Superman bolting from a phone booth to spread the good word, keep the public safe, and let your community and clients know that, unlike your competitors who are out hawking the next fast commission, you are looking out for the community.

Have you ever scrolled through news channels, the newspaper, community magazine, online articles, and the like and wondered how the same old insurance agents get the free publicity week after week? On the news again. Front page of the paper. Handing another check to some charity and getting his picture in the paper, online and plastered everywhere else he asks it to be. How do they do that?

It's simple: They ask for, and get, free publicity.

When you see something in the media, it's usually not there because some reporter had nothing better to do the prior afternoon. It is there because someone wanted it there. The articles talking about fire safety, frozen pipes, not blowing up your kitchen deep frying your Thanksgiving McTurkey Dinner, or even what The Red Hat Society is planning in Mavis' garden next Wednesday afternoon—all got there because someone wanted them there.

Now, any schmo with a laptop can fire off a press release to *The New York* Times and hope the fake news might get printed. Right. Look for that on the seventh Tuesday of next month. You need to arm your press release with the tricks-of-the-trade that will tell the reporters and editors you know what you're talking about. A real pro. A bonafide member of the club.

Some of the tricks I've learned to get my information to the top of the reporters' piles are:

- Clearly identify yourself at the top of the page and make sure you provide a working cell number and email address.

- Keep your press release to 1 to 1½ pages, never more.

- Your line spacing should be 1.5. Not 1.0 or 2.0. It's 1.5. No negotiation. It's just an unwritten rule.

- At the end of your body copy, center 3 hashtags one-and-a-half spaces below your last sentence. It's an insider's trick that tells the editor you know how to play the game.

But here's the real trick. This is the one that will get you on the Six O'Clock News...

- You ultimately want the reporter to call you on the phone and say, "Hey, John, those were some brilliant points in the press release you sent over earlier today. Could you come in and talk about _____ insurance with our audience tonight at 5:30?"

Since it's in your best interest to not look like an idiot, nor let the reporter look like one, you need to tell him what to ask you. Enclose another sheet of paper called, "Suggested Interview Questions for John Mason on Properly Insuring Straw Houses on Top of a Volcano" and give him five or six questions you want him to ask you. This just won the game for you, and since the reporter knows no more about your business than you do about writing stories and placing ads, he sees you as the expert, and you begin getting the calls when he needs advice on insurance. Your competitor's half-baked article with a picture of him holding up the bar over at Teed Off Valley Golf & Country Club will take an immediate detour to the shredder. And everybody won. The reporter has no need to research how the topic relates to insurance, and you just got to say exactly what you wanted to say to the public, for free.

CHAPTER 7
WHEN YOUR COMPETITOR JUST WON'T QUIT AND HOLDS ONTO CANCELED POLICIES LIKE A ROTTWEILER ON A BONE

It seems a growing trend in our business, more prevalent in personal lines, is that incumbent carriers are refusing to process Acord Cancellation Request/ Lost Policy Release (LPR) forms.

It's like sending them to The Bermuda Triangle; they just seem to get lost in the shuffle.

When I first started in this business back in what seems like three-weeks-after Columbus got here, I used to enjoy cramming about ten or twelve LPRs in one envelope and sending them to my competitor. The joke was on me when one of his CSRs bragged to a mutual friend that the only LPRs they x-dated were the ones from me.

That gave me a case of heartburn for about five minutes until I discovered how to get around this. It's easier than you think.

Forget sending the LPR to the other agent. If you have an email address or fax number for the carrier, send it to them directly; otherwise, mail it to the other carrier, and be sure to fill it out correctly:

a. The producer is the incumbent agent

b. Include the replacement (your) policy info

c. Attach proof of your new replacement coverage

d. And for Pete's sake, keep track, preferably electronically, of the date and time you sent this to the prior carrier.

Most of the time this will work because the LPR lands in a huge mail room or processing area along with thousands of other documents to be processed and nobody pays attention beyond making sure the form and proof of replacement coverage are correct.

Be sure to alert your new client that many agents and carriers are "forgetting" to process LPRs these days and that if they don't get confirmation of the cancellation or any refund that might be due within thirty days to let your office know. Do not, under any circumstances, encourage them to contact their old agent or carrier. You should also coach them that if they suddenly receive a lower-priced or better-coverage offer from their former provider that they should ask themselves, *If they can do it now, all of a sudden, why didn't they do it before I went shopping. How trustworthy are they?*

If your new client calls or emails and says that their cancellation was not processed, send a second request and copy your client on it. This tactic usually works, but if it doesn't, send a third notice, also copied to your client, with a cover note that says:

> *"Dear Schmuck (or former provider), As you know from the original LPR and proof of (new) coverage we mailed your office on __/__/__ and the additional copy sent on __/__/__ John & Sally Client have replaced their _____ coverage with our office. We don't understand why you're refusing to process this simple request, but if my clients don't receive confirmation of their cancellation within ten days, a complaint will be filed with the Department of Insurance. Surely, you'd prefer to process their cancellation than have to explain your actions to the commissioner's office. Thank you for your co-operation and have a nice day. Love and kisses, John Q. Newagent"*

Another way to avoid all of this on a mid-term re-write is to contact the incumbent carrier's automated direct-bill line and learning when the next installment is due, then finding out what date the client will not have coverage if a payment isn't made and coordinating your effective date with that date. Be sure not to unintentionally give them a lapse in coverage or duplicate coverage as both of these can have catastrophic results for your clients (and potentially your E&O policy). In many cases, allowing the incumbent policy to cancel for non-pay will result in a pro-rata cancellation.

A note of caution, no matter how the incumbent (now prior) policy is canceled: make sure your insured understands that if he gets a bill for earned premium due the prior carrier, that he should verify the accuracy of the cancellation date that carrier used and pay any correctly-calculated earned premium promptly to avoid collection activity which can possibly be detrimental to his credit score.

You've set the expectation that this might happen and have warned them that the sudden offer of a "new carrier" or "recent rate reduction" likely wouldn't have happened had they not shopped around. If the former agent pulls this, they'll remember your warning and that agent will look like the sleazebag you already know he is.

CHAPTER 8
GETTING YOUR AGENCY READY TO SELL TO THE HIGHEST BIDDER, LONG BEFORE THAT FIRST SHOVEL OF DIRT HITS YOU IN THE FACE

Many moons ago, you sat down with that number 2 pencil and filled in the circles on the computer-graded test you took to get your insurance license. You got your first job, wrote your first policy (mine was a $125 classic car policy, and I split the commission), then your second, then 300, and finally bought your first agency, hired a producer or two, bought another couple of agencies, put your kids through college, gave your daughter a nice wedding, joined the country club, and lived a great life.

Then it happened. One cold night last January,

your wife (I'll call her Doris) woke up at 1:49 a.m. and said, "George, I've been thinking..."

You woke up in a cold sweat because you know after 39 years of marriage that when Doris gets to thinking, it's going to cost you money. Guaranteed.

"George, you know Barbara and Tom are leaving in the morning for some Village down in Florida."

"Okay, Doris, can we talk about it tomorrow?"

"George, you know Barbara says she and Tom and half the neighbors are having a time you'd never believe. Do you know what goes on down there? We're not getting any younger, George, and if you want to stay up here and peddle policies your whole life, I'll just find someone else to go explore The Land of Swinging Seniors with."

And just like that, George had to sell his agency and retire. No time to polish the jewel and get the best price. Doris' hormones were set on central Florida, and there was no turning back. If Doris hadn't been in such a hurry to get down there to play BINGO with Diamond Don from Staten Island, maybe George would have had the time to get the maximum price for his agency.

But, oh no, Doris had been thinking....

In an optimum situation, George would have started "polishing his jewel" three to five years earlier. Rather than find every conceivable way to beat Uncle Sam out of a few bucks in creative expensing, George could have made the agency look more profitable by cutting expenses. The two new Cadillacs that he and Doris drive as well as the hot little red convertible Princess drives, all leased to the business, are expenses he's putting through the business for tax purposes but ultimately make the business appear less profitable.

Do you have perks built into your closely-held corporation? Dry cleaning as a uniform expense? Rent charges for space that doesn't exist? Family members on the payroll whose attendance is sporadic or non-existent? The boat you write off because you "sometimes take a client out" who is truthfully your deadbeat brother-in-law, and whose non-standard car policy earns you a whopping $113 annually, out fishing. Truth is, you hate the sonofabitch. Have you figured out some scheme to bring in revenue and not report it? Some of these things might (legally or illegally) reduce your taxable income, but in the long run, will significantly reduce your EBITDA to the point that potential buyers will offer less, and their lenders might not be willing to finance.

If you're running a primarily personal lines operation, are you still paying commissions to producers? Why? For certain, a savvy buyer will penalize you for this sales expense and then terminate those relationships in an effort to minimize his ongoing expenses.

Do you own the building? Do you plan to sell it to the buyers or someone else, or do you want to be a landlord to supplement your retirement? Will being a landlord work for your new lifestyle of asking people "when did you get down" and seeking out the best deal on an Early Bird Special? Are there tax implications of selling or keeping the building? If you lease, do you need to consider whether the location is next to a key anchor like the DMV? How much time is left on the lease and is it assignable?

You should consider whether you want to receive cash-up-front from the buyer, or do you want to hold a note on an installment plan or retention agreement? Are there tax implications from each?

Do you plan to work after selling the agency? Have you thought about getting a license in whatever state you're retiring to and either producing or working part-time? It sure as hell beats standing in front of Walmart greeting Toothless Tommy from Titusville—but again, what is the tax implication?

Your team has been with you for many years and has worked hard. Are they planning to stay? Is anyone planning to retire when you do? Does anyone have any ownership? Are there producers (or others) receiving commissions from the agency and how does it affect your EBITDA and resulting sale price? Are they any "special little deals" between you and any of the CSRs that the buyer (or Doris) might discover and it becomes an issue? Princess might be getting antsy for the retirement she feels she's entitled to; you remember that promise you made her late one night when you two were all alone and not exactly sober, or, in her words, dressed. You get the picture. And, are you considering any type of "thank you" for your loyal staff?

These are all things to consider when getting ready to sell your agency. Of course, Princess is just a figment of my imagination, but my point is that "special deals with staff" and any potential legal issues will complicate your sale, and likely reduce the selling price.

If you are getting ready to sell, please contact me. I have a client who is a large well-funded cash buyer of agencies, and I'll do all I can to help you get the best price for your many years of hard work.

CHAPTER 9
HOW TO FIRE A CLIENT...LEGALLY

We've all done business with them. Rude. Nasty. They treat your staff like trash. They come to your office screaming. They are verbally abusive to your team on the phone. They threaten to use the "lawyer card" or Commissioner's Office as soon as something sets them off. They don't pay their premiums, and of course, that's your fault, too, because you didn't call them and tell them to pay after they got a bill and a cancellation notice from the carrier. Or then there's Clayton the Claims Artist, who thinks the policy you sold him is the next best thing to a lottery ticket.

Where do these people come from?

I don't give a rat's patootie where they came from, but you need clients like this like you need a bad case of hemorrhoids. You don't talk to your staff that way, so why would you allow a client to do so? You don't need the toxicity of their attitude in your business, the stress they cause, or to waste your time dealing with what is usually *their* issue.

Frankly, I don't know why we call people like this clients. They are customers, not clients. I consider a client someone you share a mutually beneficial professional relationship with, and you don't treat each other that way, but that's another chapter.

There's a problem with firing these types of clients for insurance agents. Lawyers, CPAs, some types of medical professionals, realtors, and other professionals can just tell these people to take a hike, but you can't because you are not a party to their contract and don't have the legal right to cancel it. The insurance policy is a contract between the insurance carrier and the client: you just arranged it and have to service it.

Fortunately, I've only had to get rid of a few of these bad actors over the years, but it is much easier than you think.

Think about the two or three competitors you just can't stand, and who represent the same carriers you do. Fill out a Broker of Record Letter in favor of one of those agents, and mail it to the client along with a letter explaining that you can no longer service his policy, but here's another agent in the area who's taking on new clients, and would love to handle his business, at no additional cost; maybe they'll even be able to save him money. Be sure to print an envelope addressed to the insurance carrier (with postage on it) and tell him to sign it and mail it to the carrier within five business days.

This is a win-win-win.

- The client wins because he thinks he has a brand-new agent and his problems will be over. He thinks he beat you at your own game, and you'll soon be out of business.

- The carrier wins because they still have the insured. *Remember, they have the power to cancel the insured for reasons allowed by law should they so choose to.*

- Your staff wins because you've gotten rid of someone who abuses them routinely, breaks down morale in your office and wastes their time.

- You win because your staff now sees you as a hero who chose to look out for them instead of the commission you earned from this policy. (You also win for many other reasons, not the least of which is the fact that clients like this actually cost you money to service).

- And your competitor, well, he got a new client and commission and won't even know that it was a priceless little gift from you. He'll get a letter from the carrier telling him that the BOR won't be recognized until renewal but he can (depending on the carrier) service it in the meantime.

And speaking of the little gift you gave your competitor, to quote Ray Kroc, founder of McDonald's:

"If any of my competitors were drowning, I'd stick a hose in their mouth and turn on the water. It is ridiculous to call this an industry. This is not. This is rat-eat-rat, dog-eat-dog. I'll kill 'em, and I'm going to kill 'em before they kill me. You're talking about the American way of survival of the fittest."

A little tough? Yes, but not if they read this before you do. Your competitors are not your friends, and neither are abusive clients. Problem solved!

CHAPTER 10
HOW TO HELP THE LESS FORTUNATE IN YOUR COMMUNITY, GET NEW PROSPECTS IN YOUR FRONT DOOR, MASSIVE FREE PUBLICITY AND LOOK LIKE A HERO ALL OVER TOWN

Have you ever heard the pleas for help at your local food pantry and wondered how you could help? Maybe you sent a donation in during the holidays or dropped a dollar in the basket during the second collection. That was nice of you, but I've got a secret that will help those in your town who need it and put mounds of money in your pocket, all at the same time.

I've been in this industry since 1988, and I've tried it all. Classified ads. Radio ads. Showing up at the Chamber of Commerce dinner dance, those ads at the football games that don't work, shaking hands at home shows. Heck, I even spent a few years selling non-standard auto insurance off the trunk of my car.

But, there's a much better way, and you and your team members will all feel great about yourself for doing it.

Your local food pantry probably gets some help from the government, but it sure doesn't go very far in feeding all the hungry mouths desperately looking for help. And those mouths are right in your town, maybe even people you know. You might not see them in all the places you hang out, but believe me, they're out there, and they need your help.

For over 27 years, I ran a small-town independent insurance agency, and back in about 2010 or so, I was talking to an agent friend of mine in Canada who revealed the secret he'd used successfully in his town to do this.

Most towns have a Harvest Festival or some other type of event at the end of summer to celebrate the changing of the seasons. In my town, it's always been held on Columbus Day weekend, so that's when we kicked the promotion off.

We'd go to the company who does all our printing for marketing and advertising during the year and ask her to print a few thousand fliers, which, when she found out what we were doing, very graciously donated the fliers to our cause. They did their part too, as a thank you for all our printing business during the year. The fliers would announce something like this:

Local Food Pantry Desperately Needs Your Help to Feed Hancock's Less Fortunate.
The Shelves are Empty, Winter's Coming, and Your Neighbors Need Your Help NOW!
XYZ Agency Partners with Hancock Rotary Club in Annual Food Drive to Help Loaves & Fishes Food Pantry. We NEED Your Help!
For Every FULL Bag of Non-Perishable (Non-Expired) Canned or Dry Food Brought to XYZ Agency Between Columbus Day and (Date of Day Before Thanksgiving),
XYZ Will Donate $3.00 to Loaves & Fishes, and YOU GET A FREE GIFT JUST FOR BRINGING IN THE FOOD!

Now you need some "partners in crime" to pull this off. Your printer has already generously donated the printing for the fliers, but hey, you can't do it all yourself, right?

Here's where your local Rotary (or other community service organization) comes in. The service clubs love to do community service work and will gladly partner with you to get the job done. If you're not a member, ask a local club if you could come in and be a guest speaker at their meeting prior to kicking this off. These groups are always looking for speakers, and more ways to help the community, so more than likely, they'll say yes. You attend their meeting, explain what you're trying to do, and ask them if they would partner with you to help the food pantry. Make sure you take the fliers to the meeting with you.

At the meeting, ask the club president which member is in charge of community service projects. In my town, it happened to be the local Catholic priest. He then spread the word to the other churches in town and distributed fliers. The bank manager is a member of the club, and she took fliers to her bank. The postmaster did, too. Other businesses did the same. The fliers, which promoted the cause, were free publicity for my agency, all over town.

And the free advertising has begun for your agency. I sat quietly in the back of my church on Sunday listening to the priest encouraging his parishioners to bring bags of food to my agency. One week, he challenged them, "Let's see if we can bankrupt the Mason Agency this week!" The whole parish was in hysterics, and I'm sure the same thing was going on in the other churches because the bags of food started piling into our office from people who'd never set foot in the place before.

But you don't stop there.

When the generous folks in your town show up with bags of food, of course you're going to thank them, talk to them, maybe find out when their policies renew and give them a free gift. The free gift is a re-usable shopping bag smothered with ads for your agency. It's filled with the usual shiny stuff like pens, Post-it notes, etc., and information about ways you can help them protect themselves with better insurance.

Why the grocery bag? Because you'll stop in the store for a quart of milk a week or two later and see ads for your agency all over the grocery store.

Now, you're doing a great thing for the town, and more people should know, so you then create press releases and send them to local newspapers, radio stations, TV stations, etc.—and you get it on the Internet! Go to the food bank and take a video of yourself in front of the empty shelves, pleading for help, and asking people to bring bags of food to your agency, and you give that donation to the food bank. Plus, they get a free gift. People love free stuff. You post the video on Facebook and ask all your friends to share it.

Your team will get in on the action as they'll help sort, pack, and haul food to the food pantry when they're ready for it. They'll get excited and tell their friends and family, too. More help for the food pantry and more free publicity for your agency.

By Thanksgiving, you could collect a few pickup truckloads of food. Meanwhile, you keep taking pictures of the food piling in and sending them to the media and putting them on Facebook during the campaign. At the end of the campaign, get pictures of your team loading the trucks in front of your office to go to the food bank. Of course, all these pictures get released to the press and on social media.

Then, write the check with a very happy heart. Go to Kinko's and get it blown up and printed on glossy cardboard. Call the president of the Rotary (or whichever service) Club, some volunteers from the food bank, the priest who's headed to hell for hawking your agency from the pulpit, and the local media. You get them all over to your office for a photo-op with you presenting the big blown up check (and of course the real one, too). That goes to the press and on social media, too. Then keep the blown up check to hang in your lobby for your clients, visitors, and insurance company reps to see, and hopefully, it will hang right next to the one you do next year and the year after that too.

But the giving doesn't stop at Thanksgiving. You see, in working with the local food pantry, I learned that they make gift baskets for the families they help for the Christmas season. I thought to myself, *John, how you can help with that too?*

Presto! It hit me like a ton of bricks. We all travel to conferences, company meetings, continuing education classes, and vacations all year. As you travel all year, each hotel room is stocked with extra shampoo, soap, conditioner, shoe horns, sewing kits, and the like. Gather these items all year, throw them in a box somewhere, and get them to the food pantry in the fall before they build their holiday gift baskets. These items are greatly appreciated by the folks who receive them, and you're not stealing because they are figured into the cost of your hotel room! The next step is to start asking your business clients who travel to do the same thing and bring you the haul. They'll be happy to help, the less fortunate benefit, and guess what: More free publicity for your agency that might help you look like a great guy (or gal) and not just another agent trying to grab a commission.

Hopefully, you'll try this amazing community service project, which is rewarding to everyone who participates in it and truly appreciated by the members of your community who need a little extra help. Who knows, someday the tables could turn, and they could be helping you. Or maybe it will get you a few extra credits when your number comes up and St. Peter must decide about you at the Pearly Gates.

If you want to put something extra in your own pocket, visit my website www.chenangobrokers.com, and check out the products we offer that most other insurance wholesalers have no access to. We provide products in several states coast-to-coast and would love to help you help your clients. Not only that, in most cases, we can return your quotes to you in 37 minutes or less, sometimes give you online rating access, and will pay your commissions to you faster than a slot machine on steroids. Are your current wholesalers helping you, or helping you help your community?

CHAPTER 11
HOW TO USE TESTIMONIALS IN YOUR BUSINESS?

Congratulations on raising your hand and asking your clients for their honest feedback on your business. Now, what the heck do you do with them?

First, be sure to send a quick note to your client thanking him for his thoughts on your business. Mom would be proud that you're using your manners.

Where do you use testimonials to get the most bang for your buck?

Quote Packet. Don't just be the next low-priced agent trying to grab the business. When you prepare quotes, you should send a quote packet to your new prospect. I don't care if you email or snail-mail it. (I prefer snail mail because hardly anyone else uses it.) When you send your quotes, include a sheet of your testimonials, among other things. It re-affirms to your prospect that so many other people have made the same decision he is about to make.

Your Welcome Kit. If you don't know what it is, stay tuned; I'll show you that soon enough. Include a sheet of testimonials in the Welcome Kit you send out to your new clients. It drives home the point that, like hundreds of others, they have made the right decision to join your agency.

Your envelopes and letterhead. Don't overdo it here, but a good testimonial on the outside of your mailing envelopes or on the bottom of your letterhead will just keep driving the point home that many others are raving fans of your agency. The reason to "not over-do it" on the envelope is you want to make sure your clients are opening their first-class mail from you and that they don't assume this envelope is exclusively an ad. (I found out the hard way on that!)

Sales letters should include testimonials in the body of the letter (and I'd change the font, bold it up, etc.,) If you have a testimonial that matches what you're talking about in the sales letter, insert the testimonial at that point in the letter. You can also insert a buck-slip on colored paper in the envelope, or if the sales letter is being sent by email, add a sticky note with the testimonial on it.

Your websites should include both written and video testimonials from your clients. Have different testimonials for each niche or landing page. Have videos on protection, how you handled a claim, why your agency is the best choice, etc. Maybe a pop-up video testimonial?

Niches are riches! If you are a niche player, get testimonials in that niche. Don't use a testimonial that praises your homeowner's insurance rates if you are trying to write an auto body shop. Do you have a client or friend who is well-known or even famous in your niche? If so, get a testimonial, with, at a minimum, his/her picture and hopefully a video.

All other marketing whether it be newspaper, trade magazine, TV commercials, radio or even those books the phone company used to put out. What were they called? Yellow something-or-other.

You can make all the big claims you want to in marketing and advertising, but the prospect is more likely to believe what other people say about you!

CHAPTER 12
FIRST IMPRESSIONS COUNT! HERE'S HOW TO BOOST YOUR CLOSING RATIO, SHOCK & AWE YOUR PROSPECT AND IMPRESS THE HECK OUT OF YOUR CARRIERS!

Face it, quoting new business is expensive. If you don't close a prospect who calls your agency for a quote, you've wasted your time (and his) and have spent your hard-earned money on marketing, advertising, underwriting, staffing, MVRs, and so on.

You need to turn that expense into income. Now. If you don't close every deal possible, those quotes become drains on your profits from other deals you did close.

Prospects shop for insurance 24/7, every day of the year. They call around looking for the lowest price, and unfortunately, that is how many of them make their insurance buying decision. How much is it and how much a month? When those prospects call the talking lizard or other direct writers, they get a quote over the phone (or by email), but then they are dropped into a marketing funnel and dripped to for a long time.

How many independent agents do you know who send out a package of information to their prospects who ask for a quote? How many agents keep marketing to them?

Let's change that, beginning with *your* agency.

When a prospect contacts your agency seeking a quote, don't just be the next low-cost quote source for "Looky Lew" who wants to brag that he pays $1.87 a month less than the guy down the street. Insurance is intangible. Give him more than a number; send him a packet of info and educate him on what you offer as well as the benefits of doing business with your agency.

Some pointers for the Quote Packet you'll send from your agency:

- The envelope. Dress it up. A testimonial on the outside. A box printed on the envelope that says, "Here's the money-saving protection info you requested." Hand-write the prospect's address on an envelope; it's more personal and lets him know *you* are writing to him, not a computer.

- Include the quote proposal that came from your rating system or whatever proposal system you're using. Doctor it up a bit by making sure the payment plan, cross-credit discount, and all other discounts that might be available are all on the quote. If your "system" doesn't print it there, even a rubber stamp is better than nothing. Hokey? Yes, but again it's received "personally" by the prospect.

- I include a free report (white paper) on the line of business the quote is for and maybe another line you'd like to sell to the prospect. If he only wanted an auto quote, include a white paper on homeowner's coverage. Maybe umbrella, too.

- Include a sheet of testimonials and third-party endorsement letters with your quote.

- A lot of prospects are afraid of offending their current agent, and we all know the problems we incur with many agents in getting cancellations processed. Include a buck-slip on colored paper telling the prospect not to worry about canceling the old policy and how you'll take care of it in a way that won't cause hard feelings with the other agency.

- Does your agency send a monthly or quarterly newsletter? Include the most recent one.

- Does your agency give back to the community and have you gotten free publicity out of it? Include copies of what you do. (Stay tuned, we have a white paper on that, too).

- FREE GIFT. Put some "lumpy-mail" in the packets. Pen, key chain, shiny stuff, advertising your agency. Maybe a book you wrote about insurance coverage; I bet the incumbent agent hasn't written a one!

- Include a copy of your referral program if you have one (see chapter on that).

- The prospect should now be in your marketing funnel, and it's your job to create the slippery slide that leads from prospect to client to raving fan. If they don't buy now, keep marketing to them; send your newsletter, safety tips, etc., until they buy or die. The direct writers are doing it and winning, and so should you.

CHAPTER 13
WHEN CLIENTS LEAVE, YOU DON'T HAVE TO BE LIKE LITTLE BO PEEP AND HER SHEEP! HERE'S HOW…

You worked so hard to get their business. You sent them your calendar every year. You bought their kids' ad in the football roster three years ago. You thought they were with you for life.

Then, out of the blue, there it comes: THE L.P.R., otherwise known as the Cancellation Request. Wow, you didn't see that coming, and it hit you like a ton of bricks.

Maybe if you'd sent the monthly or quarterly newsletter. Touched them with a safety tip. Implemented that birthday program for clients you heard about at a seminar last year. Friended them on Facebook. Shared information to make their lives better.

But it's not too late...

I'll teach you about those nurturing and "client-cementing" tricks another time, but let's get those lost souls back in your funnel.

Yes, I call them lost souls. It's your job to find them and bring them home.

In fact, these are your most likely prospects, greater than the Internet lead, referral from Tony the mortgage broker, Susie the car saleslady, or that nice ole gal with bad perfume that Aunt Beulah plays BINGO with on Thursday nights.

They already know you and hopefully trust you, too.

Once you know they've "defected" and gone elsewhere, make sure you send a note thanking them for their past business and send them the survey to find out why they left and what it would take to get them to "come home."

Update their cancellation date in your marketing database to make that their new X-date.

Then make sure you keep sending the monthly newsletters, safety tips, cards, newspaper clippings, positive comments on their Facebook page, birthday greetings, and all the rest of your nurturing tricks. If you subscribe to a service that advises you when carriers have rate increases approved, and you know their new carrier is about to jack up their rates, send them that info and turn up the heat. And for your Sainted Aunt Agnes' sake, don't just send it to them—draw attention to it, write a note on it. I don't care if you use an orange crayon, just do it.

And remember that some people did leave because they missed a payment and are too embarrassed to call you, so it's your job to roll the red carpet out and bring 'em in. Obviously, you don't want to pursue the guy who was a constant non-pay deadbeat of a problem. But also bear in mind that sometimes people appear to cancel for non-pay because that is how their new agent gets around the barrage of tricks they sometimes face getting LPRs processed by the former carrier, or in canceling mid-term, the new agent knows a non-pay cancellation will likely be canceled pro-rata.

But remember, they won't come back if you don't take the first step. Mine your agency management system for cancellations from the past several months and cherry-pick the ones you want to get in this funnel. This is an entire marketing campaign in itself and should yield better results than marketing to prospect who don't know you.

Put on your big-boy pants and call them up prior to their renewal and ask if you can offer a quote.

If they say "yes," don't just quote them. Make sure you use your Agency Quote Package that includes free reports, testimonials, a third-party endorsement letter, free stuff, etc.

If you have a testimonial or two from clients who have left and came back, put them on a colorful, eye-catching buck-slip and call attention to it.

CHAPTER 14
USING PERSONALITY MARKETING TO FILL YOUR FUNNEL WITH LEADS, YOUR CSRS DESKS WITH NEW APPS YOUR BANK ACCOUNT WITH COLD HARD CASH

If I told you that I used to love to check into hotel rooms in strange cities and tear open the yellow pages just to see new insurance ads, you'd either tell me to get a life, a girlfriend, or wake up and realize there aren't yellow pages in hotel rooms anymore—or many other places for that matter.

But there are still many other places we still advertise in this electronic world we live in. First and foremost, our websites, social media pages, community papers, trade magazines, niche publications, video marketing, and many other advertising mediums get our messages across, but who wants to be just as boring as the competition?

People Don't Read Anymore, They Look Aa Pictures and Watch Videos. Have We Become Cavemen Again?

Why would any agent in his right mind waste money running ads that make big claims like, "We've been in business since my grandfather stole the agency from a degenerate gambler in 1939" when he could dress up in a three-piece-suit, hide underwater in his hot-tub, and on-cue, come springing out of the water asking, "Are You Sick and Tired of Getting Soaked on the High Cost of Car Insurance?" and then offer thirty seconds of in-your-face reasons to call for protection and savings and to do it *now* while his phone number and website flash on the screen. Which ad do you think will make more money? By the way, it ruined my jacket and tie, was fun, and pulled well.

Or why would an agent waste his hard-earned commission dollars running an ad offering "free quotes" in the weekly paper? First of all, did I fall asleep for the last eight months and GEICO, Progressive, and the agent down the street with the bad comb-over all started charging $39.97 for a quote? Why run an ad like that when you could pay two great kids (whose moms work for your agency) to dress up in costumes: one a pretty blond walking down the street throwing $20 bills around like chicken feed, and the other portraying that infamous green lizard chasing her down the street with a gun stealing her money. Low and behold, you come flying out of the nearest phone booth dressed up as Superman, beat up the gecko, save the blonde, give your pitch, and make the phones go wild? Which ad do you think is more effective? And which one do you think won me a Porsche to use for a year?

Personality Marketing has been around forever, but is often overlooked for the glitzy, flashy non-working copy some schlep in the compliance department thought wouldn't make the phones ring too much or make the vice president of a large insurance company quite nervous when he goes online and sees you've planted yourself on the steps of the local Catholic church, dressed up like a monk, carrying a red umbrella, and talking about religious institution insurance. No, it goes on and on: You use it to nurture your existing clients, get "lost souls" back, get yourself on TV and in the paper through press releases, your email signature, your company's printed materials, and in the videos you create to promote the charities your agency supports. You can use it in acquisition marketing, niche marketing, marketing to your carriers, new carrier marketing, new producer and CSR recruitment; obviously, you'll tailor your message depending on the intended audience.

Dare to be different. Search online for insurance ads that are different, funny, eye-catching. Do you really think the gecko or that bimbo in the white coat have lower rates for everyone or a better policy? Hell, no, they don't. But their companies employ crafty marketers who use a talking reptile or the nitwit bimbo. Oh, then there's Jake, the clean-cut, supposedly trustworthy guy you can ring up at 2:37 a.m. and break his balls over all those percentage deductibles his company sold to a trusting and unsuspecting public. Prospects respond to these ads because corporate marketers have created a persona for each of these characters that people relate to. People prefer to buy insurance from other people, not companies. You're free to search YouTube for some of the ads I recorded back in the days when I was a retail agent; search for "John Mason Insurance." Definitely search for "Vern Fonk Insurance" where my (late) friend Rob Thielke did the best job of making insurance agency ads not funny, but over-the-top hysterical.

Shapoopi!

CHAPTER 15
NOW THAT YOU'VE DISCOVERED TESTIMONIALS YOU CAN KICK BUTT WITH THEIR BIG BROTHER — INTRODUCING THE THIRD-PARTY ENDORSEMENT LETTER!

Now that you've discovered the power and credibility of using testimonials in your marketing, let's talk about testimonials on steroids.

It's great that your clients and raving fans have given you accolades and cheers for the wonderful things your agency has done for them, but why not have other insurance brokers endorsing your agency? That's right: other insurance agents, insurance company personnel, etc., endorsing your agency is even more powerful.

We all have friends in the industry that we've met at trade shows, continuing education classes, maybe belong to social media groups for agents, etc., who are not our competitors. Start out by writing an endorsement of their agency on your letterhead and send it to them with a note that says,

"Dear So and So; I'm trying to beef up my marketing by getting endorsements from non-competing agents that I can share with potential clients. I've written one for you already, and it's attached/enclosed. Would you be so kind as to write one for me and send it back by Wednesday the 12th?"

You did three things here:

1. You took advantage of the Law of Reciprocity by *giving* them something of value with the free endorsement for their own marketing.

2. You gave them a powerful marketing idea for free.

3. You set a mental deadline, and they will do their doggone best to get that letter to you by Wednesday the 12th.

And what should be in a Third-Party Endorsement letter? Use your own words, but it should be something like this:

"I've known Joe Smith of XYZ Insurance since 1997. We've worked together at numerous continuing

INTRODUCING THE THIRD-PARTY ENDORSEMENT LETTER!

education classes, trade groups, and have worked together to make insurance better for many years. I send all of my referrals in (name of area) to Joe and do so because I know the people I refer to him will be taken care of properly and professionally. If I weren't in the insurance business, I'd consider protecting my own family, home, and business with XYZ Insurance."

When prospects and clients read the Third Party Endorsement letter, their reaction should be, *"Wow, if all his customers say these things AND other insurance people say it too, maybe I should protect myself with XYZ Agency, too."*

I use the Third-Party Endorsement Letters in my Quote Packet. I've used three letters from agents in various parts of the country and have enough of them that I have rotated them for various reasons.

CHAPTER 16
IF ONLY YOUR AGENCY WAS LIKE THE HOTEL CALIFORNIA: CLIENTS WOULD CHECK-IN AND NEVER LEAVE!

Clients leave for reasons you'd sometimes never believe. There are always the usual reasons like they saved $8.37 monthly by falling for some scam from that lizard with the morals of an alley cat, their nephew's girlfriend's third cousin who you sat with at a wedding in 2011 got licensed, a claim went bad, you made some off-color remark on Facebook that pissed them off, or they didn't understand that a six-month policy wasn't a 50% rate reduction.

Then there's the big one: They missed a payment, got canceled, and were too embarrassed to come back. Why is this a biggie? Two reasons: they're usually too embarrassed to come back, and the resulting lapse probably earned them a much higher rate. If they "forgot" to pay you, they probably "forgot" to pay a few other things, their credit score deteriorated, and now they're paying more for insurance. Bottom line: they're embarrassed, and you should make it easy for them to come back.

This is easier than you think.

The first thing you need to do is send an exit survey. Ask some questions to get their honest feedback. Let them know you are sorry they left and that you'd like to know what made them unhappy enough to leave. Be sincere, and maybe even include a *hand-written* card or note. Let them know that responding is certainly optional, but you value their opinion. Keep it simple, but some of the things you should ask are:

1. If you left only due to pricing, where would we need to be price-wise for you to come back?

2. What, if anything, would you suggest we change or improve?

3. What did you like or value the most about buying insurance from us?

4. What other comments or questions do you have?

And here's the big one, the reason you're writing in the first place:

5. If we were to make the changes you suggest, would you consider doing business with us again?

The vast majority will tell you that they found something cheaper, will be touched that you cared enough to ask what happened and will say "YES" to the last question.

So They Said Yes! Now What? (Sounds too much like dating, right?)

What they said yes to was you marketing to them again and asking them back. Make sure you update your records to reflect their *cancellation date with you as their new X-date,* but don't stop there. Get them into your marketing funnel. I kept a separate database of "Lost Souls" that I would market to. I would usually send the same message I'd use for prospects, but I would edit and tailor it to former clients.

CHAPTER 17
WANT TO POUR YOUR PROFITS DOWN THE TOILET, SET UP A COMPETITOR IN YOUR OWN AGENCY, AND LATER SCRATCH YOUR HEAD WONDERING, "WHY THE HELL DID I DO THAT?" HERE'S HOW…

Over the years, I have belonged to a number of online forums, and there are a few topics that seem perpetual. One step behind the age-old question, "Are you open all day or a half a day on Thanksgiving" is the big one:

"Joe Blow Agent from down the street doesn't have the brains, bucks, or balls to run his own insurance agency, so he's going to produce personal lines for me." We're all going to get richer than Rockefeller, earn all the company trips, max out our profit sharing, and retire in the Land of Milk and Honey."

Don't bet the ranch on that one. And, just to be clear, I am *not* talking about giving your licensed CSRs a well-deserved spiff for accounts sold. You need to do that, and incentives are a horse of a different color.

Think about this for a minute. Is your agency operating at a 40% profit margin? If so, you're far ahead of the curve, but if you plan to pay this clown forty cents on the dollar for all the commission he brings in, do all the service work because Sally is there anyway, you ought to have a check-up from the neck up.

Volume without profit is like taking a leak in your shoes.

Sorry to be so blunt, but that's the way it is. I made this mistake, so I'm telling you not to. Hundreds of thousands of dollars later, I know better. I'll just cut to the chase and tell you why.

- Personal lines do not generate, in most cases, the type of commission revenue that commercial lines do. You pay Sally and Betty to handle all the service on it, (hoping to make that 40% bottom line), but instead, you're going to pay forty cents of every dollar to that dumb-like-a-fox clown who sees you as his own private service center. Notice, you've now hired Betty to help Sally to handle the new business you're paying through the nose for.

- Why, for God's sake, would you set up a competitor in your own agency? You read that right: <u>a competitor</u>. You are competing for that same customer directly with that guy you've set up a service center for. I like Santa Claus and the Easter Bunny too.

- After a while, Sally and Betty begin to wonder, "Why do we have to do all of his work? Isn't he supposed to handle all his own apps, changes, and the like?" On the flip side, when clients can so easily go online with other providers and purchase insurance, why would he want to add an extra step with your producer?

- Oh, and those %*&^@#*! "back-pay" lists. They'll show up every couple of months with a list, "Hey, John, I don't mean to bring this up, but Beulah Jones traded her '87 Buick for a brand new Hyundai last April and got full coverage, and I never got paid for the endorsement." They'll have about 26 more of these on their list and want you to look into it. Where's the Tylenol? (This in itself is a compelling reason why you reconcile direct bill commissions and use your agency management system for all accounting.)

- So this arrangement goes on for a few years, then you begin to wonder, *What happens if my producer takes his book to another broker, dies, or retires while I'm still here servicing his book?* One day after work, you sit down with this clown in a private meeting with John Barleycorn and try to come up with a solution. Well, the not-so-dumb-fox comes back to you about a week later and suggests you sign some sort of a buyout agreement giving him ownership of his book. Be careful because now the sonofabitch will never go away. You sign it, relieved that you've "locked him in" and forget about it. A few years later, you begin hearing what the other old farts are doing down at The Villages and sell your agency. Guess who is going to be so happy to congratulate you on the sale and remind you that his book is *his*, and he needs to be bought out. Of course, most savvy buyers will want him out of the picture, too. (This can and should be avoided if you still decide to hire a personal lines producer after reading this.)

- "But I'll make it up with contingency." Yeah right, and the tooth fairy showed up with Kennedy half dollars and shoved 'em under your pillow when you were five, too. Never, and I mean *never* bank on contingency. Just last December, I had a million-dollar homeowner's loss that sent a contingency down the tubes faster than a fat kid at an all-you-can-eat buffet. And, I didn't know about it until January 15.

Don't beat yourself up for having this idea. Just don't do it. Between us, before I knew better twenty-something years ago, I'd spend Sunday afternoons typing the Acord home and auto apps at home for my producer to go out and close her deals! Can you imagine?

But There's An Easier, and Cheaper, Way To Sell Personal Lines!

There's nothing wrong with selling personal lines, and I've made a boatload of money doing just that, and from a very small town in the middle of nowhere.

Instead of paying that ne'er-do-well-scoundrel down the road, why not invest in marketing systems for your own agency that drives prospects to the phone or your website? Think about it; rather than paying that idiot forty percent of the revenue he brings in *plus* the cost of servicing it, why not invest in marketing that will drive prospects into your marketing funnel for a much lower cost and then continue to invest in those relationships by nurturing those relationships and cementing those them forever?

ABOUT THE AUTHOR

John Mason fell into the insurance industry in 1988 in a poor town in the middle of nowhere in upstate New York. He had drive and a dream, but no money, no customers, and no insurance knowledge. Over the next few years, he sold personal lines, earned his CIC, and bought a few agencies.

In the late 1990s, he began studying marketing, bought a small wholesale brokerage, and continued to expand his business. In the early 2000s, he began to aggressively grow his businesses, entering neighboring states, and earning the largest contingencies ever paid by one of America's largest insurance carriers for a few years in a row. In 2007, he expanded his growing insurance business into the New York City area and purchased five brokerages in the Bronx over the next four years.

During this time, he began teaching seminars on agency marketing and management and also did international one-on-one consulting for agencies who wanted to grow and/or become more profitable.

In 2014, he decided to slow down to enjoy life in the Caribbean and focus solely on his wholesale business. He sold all of his retail agencies over the course of the next two years and continues to focus on his ever-growing wholesale brokerage and continues to (selectively) offer one-on-one consulting services to agencies who are looking to grow. Consulting services can be requested by emailing him at jmason@chenangobrokers.com

Made in the
USA
Middletown, DE